PINE KNOWING PAIN

BOOKS BY MARTIN JANELLO

LIVE KNOWING LIFE
ISBN 978-0-9910649-6-0 (Paperback)
ISBN 978-0-9983020-2-7 (Kindle)

LOVE KNOWING LOVE
ISBN 978-0-9910649-7-7 (Paperback)
ISBN 978-0-9983020-3-4 (Kindle)

PINE KNOWING PAIN
ISBN 978-0-9910649-5-3 (Paperback)
ISBN 978-0-9983020-6-5 (Kindle)

SHINE KNOWING SHAME
ISBN 978-0-9983020-4-1 (Paperback)
ISBN 978-0-9983020-7-2 (Kindle)

CLIMB KNOWING AIM
ISBN 978-0-9983020-5-8 (Paperback)
ISBN 978-0-9983020-8-9 (Kindle)

KNOWING WON'T LET DARKNESS REIGN
ISBN 978-0-9983020-1-0 (Paperback)
ISBN 978-0-9983020-9-6 (Kindle)

PHILOSOPHY OF HAPPINESS
ISBN 978-0-9910649-0-8 (Hardcover)
ISBN 978-0-9910649-8-4 (Paperback, Pt. 1)
ISBN 978-0-9910649-9-1 (Paperback, Pt. 2)
ISBN 978-0-9910649-1-5 (PDF E-book)
ISBN 978-0-9910649-2-2 (Kindle)
ISBN 978-0-9910649-3-9 (EPUB)

PHILOSOPHIC REFLECTIONS
ISBN 978-0-9910649-4-6 (PDF E-book)

PINE KNOWING PAIN

PHILOSOPHICAL QUOTES & POEMS

MARTIN JANELLO

Copyright © 2016 by Martin Janello
All rights reserved

No part of this book may be reproduced or transmitted,
in any form or by any means, electronic,
mechanical, or otherwise,
without prior written permission from its copyright owner

Cover, book design, and artwork by Martin Janello

Published by Palioxis Publishing

Palioxis, Palioxis Publishing,
and the Palioxis Publishing colophon
are trademarks owned by Martin Janello

Publisher website:
www.palioxis.com

Book website:
www.philosophyofhappiness.com

ISBN 978-0-9910649-5-3

First Edition

CONTENTS

I. QUOTES	1
II. STILLBORN LOVE	35
III. LOVE ANTICIPATED	59
IV. LOVE PRESENT	85
V. LOST LOVE	111
VI. DARKNESS	129
VII. POETIC ESSENCE	145
VIII. ART OF LIFE	161
IX. TRUST AND DOUBT	179
X. FICTION AND REALITY	201

This book is dedicated
to
those who
cherish life
beyond the pain

I.
QUOTES

I. QUOTES

passive aggression
and lack of care
do more harm
than confrontation

i like to watch candles
because they remind me
that we can burn showing
warmth light and grace

We call those who do not give up
against great odds principled
geniuses if they succeed and tragic
fools if they fail.

principled people
may get broken
others get by
being bent and subdued

another day
running down the meter
meaning competing
with energy lost

How many of us keep asking whether
they do everything possible to avail
themselves of happiness and then
keep acting on this insight?

I. QUOTES

we must not dwell
where the heart is contained

we cannot help those
who won't pay attention

the world could be healed
if we came to our aid
assisting one another

we lift from the past
to reach for the future

at times we use

goodbyes to others

seeking to separate

parts of ourselves

we stand up against gravity

yet also value its grounding

many conditions are like that

with the setting of the sun

review the gifts of day

make plans

for what you would have done

had time not slipped away

I. QUOTES

the primary rule of education
is learning to feel and show
love for the world

We sometimes mistake trite and true.

attention to signs
rarely anything
grabs us unannounced

ponder and search
how to meet your self

Those sailing through are not trained
to deal with adversity.

Loving only yourself leaves your
capacities sadly underutilized.

some day soon
it might fall back on knights
defending the weak to the grave

wanting our life to rhyme
sometimes leads to forced endings

I. QUOTES

Be in you and everything else.

Every place reflects its inhabitants'
souls - sooner or later.

we are destined
to be deconstructed
and reassembled by love

those who would betray us
can only hurt us
if we betray first ourselves to them

Care who shapes your memories.

all worthwhile roads
cross one another

societies like
their philosophers dead
evading compelling reproach

Those trying to make all their dreams
come true must have either selective
memory or a craving for punishment.

I. QUOTES

power's inherent in sensitive souls
their warmth eventually melts the ice
as surely as spring in moderate zones
if they keep and shine their lights

rock bottom
grants opportunity
to get up
and take a stand

Sayings quoted a million times or
coined by someone we admire may
contain truth. Still we must not
accept them without critical inquiry.

the only fair contest
is within you
proving you're better
than before

give replace take
love replace hate
work replace fate

what if
the cockroach you just killed
would have given rise
to a new zenith of nature
after humanity is gone

I. QUOTES

We can end all considerations
whether glasses are half full or empty
by changing to smaller glasses.

we may have reasons
to curse our lives
but we would only
sentence ourselves

extending our light
deep into the night
we fail to experience
morning's promise
and run to catch up all day

some desire eternal night

some wish for endless day

i love balance of dark and light

but not in a sense of gray

if we would only

acknowledge people

and make them feel

they matter to us

exceeding coexistence

truly connected

we would not bear

the suffering of others

I. QUOTES

The epitome of stupidity is believing
others are or have been much smarter
and following them on that basis.

don't hold a speech
just talk to people

frustration endeavors seducing us
to lower appropriate standards

having no reason to be one's friend
thus is true friendship defined

life is cruel

is stating a fact

what makes it so

causes reason to act

a man attempting

control of a woman

is like a dog

trying to train a cat

happiness

is not easily found

defining our goals

in a negative fashion

I. QUOTES

scientists claim
life runs in circles
i have proof
because my life does

humans without restraint
are prone to exert abuse
but so are humans
in charge of such restraint

A most intractable issue of humanity
is that we become frustrated when we
cannot reach our objectives, but also
after we have accomplished them.

i will not follow
who won't follow me
loathe disinterested vanity

the clueless and those of depravity
and others who won't dare trying
worsen this planet's gravity
but cannot keep us from flying

It is revealing and self-defeating how little interest many philosophical thinkers show in the ideas of others, hoping this will keep their mental houses of cards unscathed.

I. QUOTES

embracing the earth
should be natural
after all
she's our mother

running out
of pictures of you
gives you a chance
to look at yourself

we may say myths
are unreal stories
but tell them for reasons
telling on us

We are old when we believe or realize
we can no longer escape our past.

the only conditions able to haunt us
are undead snippets of ourselves

Too much has never happened to do
the right thing.

we are on this earth
not to seek emptiness
but harmonious fulfillment

we deem ourselves civilized
when we don't physically abuse
but are still primitive brutes
if we don't equally mind
mental pain we inflict

Those calling people stupid often
overlook that many pretend so they
can avoid facing other shortcomings.

don't trouble yourself
forming words to impress me
if you're not ready
to listen as well

We are partial to confirmations of our views because they prove acumen. However, we must seek all three by rigorous questioning to live a life of truth and best chances for happiness.

When we look for reasons to help other than need, we aim to generally justify our denial of assistance.

most people can't stand
being just with themselves
and tensely withdraw
from this uncharted land

I. QUOTES

we may change manners
looks stories friends cars
we still have to live
with who we are

we fight others fearing
there is not enough
when this is the reason
we and they are lacking

Being loved grants power to make
people comply. Loving grants the
attitude to not take advantage
of that power.

free kind words can lighten
familiar and unknown woe
why then do heart purses tighten
preventing love to flow

The secret of success generally lies in
climbing without a fear of heights
while being aware of their presence.

we can establish eden
if we learn of harmony
within ourselves
with others
and nature

I. QUOTES

Some of the most forbidding limits
and treacherous derailments we meet
are those we set for ourselves.

why give more attention
to those who give us less

There is an end to everything, even to
ends when they are forgotten.

Pretentiousness reveals fear of not
being enough.

we had a look at the open door
but feasible paths are such a bore
blocked access compels our interest

practice steadfast calm and kindness
or let confusion and evil win

The world feels to you like you do.

beauty and wit
matched by
grace and grit

I. QUOTES

a multitude of parallel universes
can be easily confirmed
by sampling the mindsets of people

gold you hoard
survives you cold
inheritors glad it is freed

Still too many looking for a friend.

what am i is a senseless question
better to ask what effect do i have

expecting concepts to rhyme

may reflect childish attitudes

toward language liberty and logic

all the more magical is it if they do

teaching children

the use of words

so they won't use fists

or one day swords

some say in this age

male traits are outdated

i say they are not

developed enough

We must fight fears, not one another.

how many clothing customs
are instruments of repression

to not express our pain
and its sources
inserts them even deeper

Cultures valuing good looks pressure their members to take care of their bodies. So much for superficiality.

programmed relief

arrives with buying

dour replacement

for purpose in life

humanity stoops

to monstrosities

it then spends most energy

fighting

a frequent blunder

with feeling special

is the assumption

that others are not

I. QUOTES

freedom becomes real
when we stop buying
what we are sold
without consideration

hand in hand
by mutual respect
prevents them
from picking up weapons

Many deem dealing with things easier than dealing with people. They may therefore also prefer to deal with people as or through things.

Most crucial choices are disarmingly simple. Some of us complicate them to avoid or delay them being made.

we buy better televisions
in hopes they improve
our programming

catching the flow
with varied utensils
truth is
we can't hold anything
not even ourselves
for very long

I. QUOTES

problems are like slippery eels
that live in morasses of souls
we must rise till we free our heels
to sunlight above these shoals

false virtue
hounds virtuosity
envious
of life's enjoyment

When we deem new beginnings
impossible or too arduous, we resist
them, aiming to defeat ourselves in
an infight between fear and hope.

A deeper reason many are afraid of the rise of artificial intelligence is that its programming forces us to reflect on, comprehend, and justify or adjust our mental and behavioral patterns.

We are taught to love everyone. But if we told or showed everybody we love them, we would be judged insane.

The worst self-inflicted torture is halting and fixing your life waiting for someone to return your love. Move on and maybe revisit if you still care.

II.
STILLBORN LOVE

II. STILLBORN LOVE

disturbances run
through her fairest complexion
i speak but she is not here with me

afraid to force fate
he fails to call
until it's too late

the girl who stopped my heart
when she stepped off the train
has me walking her car
in dreams ghostlike in vain
one day she might be mine
when i travel back in time

she distanced herself
before he withdrew
or caused love enough
to hurt her

the prettiest girl i had ever met
sent signals to me she could be had
i didn't hold back but could hardly be
life had not blossomed me yet

she does not know you
and still carries chills
from past disappointments
with also a man

II. STILLBORN LOVE

he could not believe
he did not kiss her back
having reserved his love for so long

when you are
there is no me
when i am
there is no you
the universe planned our separation
we still can imagine our love

he frantically tried
slipping back into dream
to meet the love of his life

after she tells him

that he's a joke

he still does not abandon all hope

since women assert

in matters of love

the attraction of men

who make them laugh

she spoke softly

another language

though she knew

i was not of her tribe

kissed my neck

and rushed away

saving me

from her sanguine bite

II. STILLBORN LOVE

k she muttered
when he announced
how thrilled he was to meet her

she acts as if he were invisible
so she won't get caught in his gaze

he thought he could read her
by captions of similar stories

she brashly called herself a diva
ugliest beauty i ever met

stripped of all self-respect

had no regard

for those who loved him either

take me she begged

since she had decided

she did not want herself anymore

don't think of me

as latent lover

consider us more

like sister and brother

that is the only way

we can be friends

II. STILLBORN LOVE

how many she baits
with shallow tackle
only got worse
in the digital sphere

bad fortune would have it
they missed each other
colliding instead
with some other saps

last time he checked
he still did not like her
but will keep sampling
at least few more times

focused so much
on those who won't love us
neglecting to see
the ones who do
engrossed so deeply
in those we care for
failing to mind
who else needs our love

i plan on being happy one day
she said not including me

accept some love
will never happen

II. STILLBORN LOVE

she tried and tried again and again
then grasping the meaning of never
some elements have to stay apart
that once were united at the start

She made men compete for her like
she was a grand prize. Predictably,
the one who finally won her sought
revenge for his humiliation.

love me
nerves flesh blood heart
wanted to scream
but she fell silent seeing no use

i got away

with one blue eye

you don't want to see

the other guy

who's living with her now

i've always loved you

the saddest words

when they come as a surprise

i try to remember

her name or face

yet all that remains

is her gentle demeanor

II. STILLBORN LOVE

reunion

she says you could have had me

still not the kind of love i want

go away or stay

he'll never be with you

it's almost like

he doesn't need love

at least not your kind

he typed he did not think

she was real

she wrote nowadays

that does not matter

she jealously guarded her advantages
so when i could not be with her
she pretended not to care

mistreats him
for reminding her
of one she loved in pain
contending with this phantom
he proves to be the same

you know well
she won't fall for you
still you must keep on
tirelessly hoping

II. STILLBORN LOVE

taking a seat beside me at the bar
she tells me she's a virgo
i'm unsure how much latin she knows

detests him for knowing
where she had come from
blames on him pain
from irrational shame

between her thinking
she is too good
and his supposition
he's not good enough
they make a perfect couple

once deemed herself
much too dear for him
seeing him now she's considering
fair trade for depreciating beauty

he used to brag
that he had had her
but she left a hook in his heart
he's been trying to pull out ever since

she calls him to say
she can't talk anymore
her fiancé
won't allow male friends

II. STILLBORN LOVE

the first sign she sent me
was plain to see
she did not care
how i take my tea

wandering mazes of icy sharp edges
steeling our souls and locking love in
we become contemptible wretches
for whom defrosting's an ultimate sin

one evening i was stuck at her flat
weather had turned unexpectedly bad
she offered me sleeping on the floor
foretelling the life i would have had

he was just playing
to win a friend's bet
and did not expect
to be mate checked

lost love letter
stamped hundred years ago
sepia emotions
still unfulfilled

her prettiness
cheapened by pettiness
and obstinate claims
for admiration

II. STILLBORN LOVE

just moved-in girlfriend
despite her small size
thoroughly gives me the creep
for cutting her hair
she says otherwise
would strangle us in our sleep

she never answered any letters
i hoped she would know
i was too shy to send

her looks outdo
the beauty of her heart
a temporary problem

proclaims without prompting

i am not her type

as if that were to be aspired

walking spring forests

longing for you

walking fall forests

nothing's come true

brace for a cold heart winter

first she besets him

with hints of her liking

then laughs it off

as he starts to believe

II. STILLBORN LOVE

i met her when all else had gone
fighting two thousand miles of winter
to get to an unaffected zone
but all we found was callous sinter
collapsing she cursed me to die alone

tell him your dreams
none will matter a thing
he only wants to please you
so you'll be moved to please him

she had a great gift
for giving advice
taking it was her problem

wild and undomesticated
his heart tried to break
from her confining love
with every run into her fences
barbed wire ripped more shreds

angelic presence
apricot butt
he asked her to meet him
but she answered not

this was your test
she said after asking
for my opinion on animal trials

II. STILLBORN LOVE

she starts to judge men
with a ten in her mind
then orderly scans for deductions

she looked to warm
her frozen hands
that's how the whole thing
got started and ends

he searched for love
or waited for it
depending on
which option
would not work

i never met her
but wondered why
she was so closed
in both directions
her melancholy moved me
romantic forsaken love

she called him selfish
as he admitted
he loved her most for loving him

he quietly waits
for permission of passion
accepting her rules of engagement

III.
LOVE
ANTICIPATED

III. LOVE ANTICIPATED

she's taken over
my head heart and nerves
no part of me left that isn't hers
and still she begs me to take her

sensitive words
and the way you say them
bring to light
the core of my being

dancing with her
was already bliss
when she sighed
hold me closer than this

she is not easily impressed
the least by people who try

don't slouch
said her mother
if you want a man
child lessons
she aims to unlearn
if she can

i could not stand how much
you made me need you
till you said you desperately
needed me too

III. LOVE ANTICIPATED

don't fall for me

she warned the stranger

i have no remorse

give no guarantees

i'll take that risk

despite the danger

attraction will force

us both to our knees

upset nobody will listen to her

i do

cries nobody fathoms her pain

i try

resigned nobody loves her

i might

but i am nobody to her

and love snarked at me
i'll be there in time
worry instead
about getting ready

his heart was not cold
just well preserved
for incidents yet to come

what i've lost or never had
saved gained or made
wished relished or regretted
you say you want to embrace it all
and that you will never leave

III. LOVE ANTICIPATED

tired but too wound
for sleep to set in
thoughts of you racing
through my veins

he recalled her
smelling like a puppy
her scent had changed
being all grown up

i'd like to make up for the years
someone else left you in tears
by lifting you up so high
you will miss to cry

however you use your charm and wit
she will not commit
until there's enough
of you to hold on to

had you in mind
since before i met you
still you remain undefined

waiting for you
to come around
it suddenly hit me
we're going in circles
missing the point of love

III. LOVE ANTICIPATED

the girl who would not talk to me
thought i would not talk to her

how to begin to speak to someone
with whom you imagine
the rest of your life

i need you to make peace in me
but first tease me out of my mind

her presence makes me
consciously breathe

is that so she laughed

when i told to her face

i liked other parts of her body too

brushing my arm

with the back of two fingers

she asked are you feeling this

torturing me until i would admit

my nerves were all concurrently lit

dreamed i heard an angel's wings

batting the air with force

did she come to encourage sins

or fill me with remorse

III. LOVE ANTICIPATED

my speaking to her
seemed like presumption
but she later said
she was hoping for that

i had a dream
long before i met you
that falling in love
i'd remember this dream

how did you know
she keeps on asking
when will she see
i can feel her heart

she says i've awakened

deep unknown emotions

protective naked and ferocious

in stirrings of company

lone in my world

i cannot help dreaming of you

some tell him he's naive

to hold on to the belief

that he can find

his counterpart

the kind of person

who knows him by heart

III. LOVE ANTICIPATED

deeming herself too cold for comfort
seeking his warmth at the risk of fire

she prophesies
she'll change my mind
i'll hand it over
to rejoin my heart

lone castle
tower watchman
buffeted
by icy storms
holding out
for signs of love

she squinted and smiled
when i played her a lick
fueling my imagination

bolted down
by her divine lightning
while my heart was shouting
run talk to her

locked in dead night
she unearthed me
i fear her love light
will sear and blight
proving me unworthy

III. LOVE ANTICIPATED

she calls me honey
though we've just met
i bet she says that
to all guys at the diner

she opens the door
in her underwear
to not keep me waiting
while she's getting dressed

barely the nerve
to go and ask her
between elation
and total disaster

you admit to be
out of your element
here in the wild
but more than eager
becoming part of mine

each time he whispers
in her ear
that side of her body
gets goosebumps

she would be perpetually haunted
with finding a man
who would know what she wanted

III. LOVE ANTICIPATED

she whispered in french
before she kissed me
i wish i had paid more
attention in school

the most magical love
has not yet taken aim

she momentarily forgot
the purpose of her search
oh yes her heart
it must be here somewhere
in a lock box
safe from being crushed

she never wants to stay
past midnight
that's why i call her
my little pumpkin

the way she focused
on her meals
made him suspect
her a capable lover

he only hints
at his dreams of the one
so he'll recognize
a true soul's kinship

III. LOVE ANTICIPATED

she wasn't ready for love

first wanted to

lose weight

clean up

tan

do hair

makeup

buy that dress

but boy was she ready for him

she stayed helping me clear the table

after a party at the stable

first thought she

wanted lessons riding horses

yet it was me

who wound up taking courses

the way you caressed
the flower i found
fills me with hope
our love will abound

his staunch resistance
was reason enough
for her to drop shame
and sunbathe buff

what would he not do
to be with her
the list of such actions
kept shortening

III. LOVE ANTICIPATED

why is she crying
when i love her
she tells me
she is not used to this

no my love
that will not work
is this an omen
assembling their bed

he could love you
for you are lovely
but wonders
what it would do to you

reading my half-finished script
she got caught up in my story

can't stay or go
till i know your heart

she asked to leave it all to her
if she was to give herself to him

she wore a double breasted suit
on which the top buttons
looked awfully cute

III. LOVE ANTICIPATED

finding the word horsepower racy
she dresses for our test drives lacy

molten fabric contouring her shapes
she protests it's freezing in here

why does she whisper in my ear
even when we are alone

thinking of you
though you said i shouldn't
my heart's not taking orders well

i steal your glances
not giving them back
until you ask me why

she secretly wished
he'd touch more of her skin
the windstorm obliged like a lover

her presence
makes my blood race
and she's the only cure
her absence
makes my heart ache
and she's the only cure

III. LOVE ANTICIPATED

having made love to you all day
it struck me not having put away
the milk i bought this morning
lots of spoiled dairy is dawning

there she's again
in this crazy dream
he cannot shake
sleeping or waking

she dropped by for apologizing
but did not find the conditions right
he's smart enough for recognizing
the entire matter's not worth a fight

she said i feel cold
he took off his jacket
and threw it away
to feel closer to her

i'm leaving she said
it all up to you
how much you want me
in your life

she kept her girlfriends
separate from me
concerned they would enter
in competition

IV.
LOVE
PRESENT

IV. LOVE PRESENT

to love her enough
and want to be with her
i have to be me always
separate from her

riding its waves
until we let go
this strangest of oceans
more us than we know

though their friends warned them
of differences
they fit together
like plus and minus

your love has let me again be strong
when you met me i was almost gone
fighting the rotten things people do

grey morning clouds
muddled cotton sheets
we are still soaked
by last night's torrent

she wants wild gales
of warm wind and rain
run lie and whirl with them untame
without any care and free of shame
she's overjoyed he feels the same

IV. LOVE PRESENT

she came with love
wide as the horizon
and deep as the sky
focused on his heart

thought i woke up
and not with you
only a nightmare
not yet come true

she keeps wanting
a sapphire ring
but it would pale
against her eyes

no more suffering

cold autumn sundays

pacing the park

like a mobile scarecrow

i want to save you

like a perfect bowl of ice cream

but then pretend you'd quickly melt

that the love we have for each other

will not outlast us is no bother

because it's not meant for anyone else

still it makes us feel we'd rather

see an end to humankind's hells

IV. LOVE PRESENT

riding out beyond the moat
ready to lay down his life
covering like a cavalier's coat
for her and their unborn
to walk through the strife

she never noticed
her eyes had this color
until he described their beauty

the beach changes colors
for lovers walking
brushing them softly
with evening mist

our embrace

frees time and space

and their implications

from our minds

the way we move

sense and touch each other

makes words seem like

ruptures in conversation

gushing ideas of who we are

spring from the fountain of here

sharing our flow of consciousness

until we both shed a tear

IV. LOVE PRESENT

when loving someone
is something you have to
not because love
you receive in return

let us dream of
dank autumn weekends
and what we will do
after candles are lit

my only regret
i met you not earlier
experience instead
i'd gladly give

the world with her
had a different light
glowing warm from within

one partial complaint
in his loving bliss
she makes more of everything
than it is

strange
what she asked him
to do to her
was exactly
what he had in mind

IV. LOVE PRESENT

his impact frightened her
she did not know
how she could live without him

you calm me
to weather any storm
because i am sheltered
in your love

they are each other's mirrors
reflections of nothing beyond
this might appear like perfect love
but will their light tire
from traveling between them

leaving much to be desired
the secret to my loving you

whoever i am you are the other
we're melting each other's mold

she is a reel
with my every nerve attached

the way she wears her long silken hair
dream catcher for many admiring her
my folded night veil that will not tear

IV. LOVE PRESENT

loving you

is giving me showers

hot and cold

in this simple one-room house

with one light bulb

over a wooden table

two chairs and our bed

i find a warm home

saving me from bitter naught

that riff you do with your hair

when i'm watching

is making me want to stay

cold mornings are my favorite threat
i overcome with you in bed

you say you don't want flowers
but i dream of them surrounding you

when missing us
is the worst emotion

loving a woman
one must respect
the girl that is part of her

IV. LOVE PRESENT

i had long forgotten
how genial life could be
when she opened judgment
and loving arms to me

don't let me say
how much i love you
our time might end
with it left unshown

how can this woman be so strange
and yet be so familiar
maybe i'm used to the idea
i'll be exploring her forever

i am wild
don't let clowns on my back
lions yield when i lower my head
she has tamed me but i am no pet
we're wild together since we met

as long as there's you
in this world for me
i'm not giving up on it

my soul and body
and yours in return
belong to each other
thus we won't yearn

IV. LOVE PRESENT

make with me jam
from this bed of roses
kiss me so we chafe
the sides of our noses
love me until we fall apart

listen to music my fingers make
when you're not here
to let them play you

we know nothing about each other
save all our senses' burning passions
don't let this mystery painfully hover
and leave at rest past cold dead ashes

she says i'm beautiful for you
suspending everyone enchanted
but i only know really what it means

she is unconsciously lovely
i'm always aware of that

the ways we fit so perfectly together
although we were made entirely apart

you being you in my presence
unaware of what you give

IV. LOVE PRESENT

once in a while
pretend not to know her
contend for her love
like you did the first time

streaks of sunrise
closed shutters let through
prove to the eyes
my dreams have come true

if you ask me
what matters true
just after being
it's being with you

pull gray sky down
enshrouding us
to hide or find
in its matting stillness

how she flung her arms
and flew into mine
i wish i could come back forever

he takes her out
of all she had
lived or hoped for
ecstasy now
is her standard of living

IV. LOVE PRESENT

volumes of truth
expressed by our eyes
every time
it comes to goodbyes

you never lose a love
whose tears
have joined with yours

love's frictions
grinding them raw
still they won't quit
holding out
for worthwhile soothing

you make me wish
for winter storms
so we build a fire
with each other

the purpose of love
is not to be one
but staying two
engaged in a dance

out of paths
to move even closer
they took distance
and new approaches

IV. LOVE PRESENT

they fell in love
between universes
welding transitions
with heat from their union

don't you know
after all this time
that love you give
increases thine

you never frown at or doubt me
nor are embarrassed by what i am
you claim it's because you love me
but loving yourself is how it began

why did we recognize each other
not having known of us before
why did our bodies and souls entwine
why do i have you and want you more

what will you do
when the rush is over
he says with her
it never will

loving you
i feel time fast-forwards
and yet again strangely
also stands still

IV. LOVE PRESENT

deepest desert

sands grow paler

full moon gold

star sprinkled night

two folding chairs

silver bullet trailer

pink flamingo guards

you say alright

you just think

the bee said

i care for you

because i'm attentive

collecting your honey

that's what love is

the flower responded

You make telling me unnecessary.

i did not know what tenderness was
until i let you touch my heart

hold on to me
safe in the vessel of our love
throughout the rapids of life

love returned without camouflage
to dance by the skins
of her body and soul

V. LOST LOVE

V. LOST LOVE

desiccant frost beyond degrees
what once was flexile
now brittly splintered

he never got to say goodbye
but shown her such love
it did not matter

nothing between them
could have this effect
some dreadful cause
made her not come back
how he wished he were
the reason instead

like gaudy wallpaper
or a long-broken chair
she could not stand him
to be still there

drawing in the breath you give me
with this last impassioned kiss

her first few cries
he consoled with lies
later he'd just wait
for them to go by
until she had finally
run out of tears

V. LOST LOVE

she used the vase

as a crystal hammer

how could he presume

roses undo betrayal

of all miserable relations

he had left

he thought

he should have left sooner

surrounded by him

a heavy mantle

she shed to be weightless

and dance like the air

your disinterest

made me go on without you

now you begrudge i relish freedom

salt of the sea

i taste without you

reminds me of times

i made you cry

sparing me the ruinous truth

that your love was fading away

you set me up

deeply falling from love

i went on believing still existed

V. LOST LOVE

listening to old italian pop
your favorite
i briefly was that summer

alright he said
we're good for now
that's when she knew
it had to end

anything returning you
i'd dedicate my life to it
had no idea
when you were with me
i would have lived in fear

so that's how it feels

when hope is gone

what a strange relief

i'll go on loving

the picture of you

i saved from the fire

you set to my heart

i know what it feels like

when your heart melts to the ground

chills freeze your body's motions

you witness yourself hurting

like a close friend unable to cry

V. LOST LOVE

selling her out for another future
was a goodbye he thought
but this unborn love life
would haunt him forever

looking up
at your bedroom window
made me want to change history

played admiration
how i took the news
eased the pain only for her
angry she could still hoodwink me
into her notion of strength

if she keeps insisting
that i am wrong
she'll have to agree
that i am gone

i must have failed
what she expected
but will never know
i should have guessed

when parts of my heart
remained unbroken
you returned
to shatter the rest

V. LOST LOVE

cold light upon me

today i die

to love some other time

on leave

from preapproved life

he stopped by

to pay respects

to aging aspirations

phone call

disconnected

she needs to go

i know there will be no later

for you it counts more
to tell who left whom
than honoring we had love

dreams saw her alone
on the deck of a ship
directing it with her love
she wanted to hit
sharp rocks with it
and fly away as a dove

take it from me
how beautiful you are
by showing me your ugly side

V. LOST LOVE

coming to grips with your leaving
silent while our hands
are still talking to each other
not finding much solace thinking
that pictures of us
will outlast our company
a dreadful moment worse than dying
and still i wish it would not end

basket of pens and whimsical trinkets
so many still lifes of her existence

he scolded her for his feeling cold
but would not let her warm him

she left me jaded
encased in the concrete
of real life lost love experience

she wished he would go
without dulling the knife
by taking pains to ease the cut

it's like you have all
but forgotten me
or never embraced
the meaning of we
while i'm still here
desperately trying

V. LOST LOVE

she loved him for some differences
but only stingily humored the rest
becoming accustomed to his favors
she started viewing him as a pest

once confident
they were destiny
since love fell flat
rustling restlessly
conjuring ways
to return to freedom

it was not me who disappointed
just the vision she had of me

your pride made you leave
mine had me agreeing

tomorrow you'll go on without me
and soon will deny i was ever there

pleading he never meant to hurt her
meaningless like so much he had said

meals they ate
while she was his mate
now poisoned retroactively

V. LOST LOVE

she boxed my music and model plane
the only things i did not let her touch
and put them labeled with my name
by the curb in hammering rain

resenting each other
for broken dreams
convenient distraction
from their own failures

tomorrow
i shall let you go forever
and then wait forever
for you to come back

why do true lovers
turn into strangers
cutting their feet off
to walk away

i don't care anymore
about what you said
i should let go
is this enough to have us back

he asked passers-by
if they had seen her
in disbelief
she would just leave

VI.
DARKNESS

VI. DARKNESS

distant from life

sitting in her chair

thin parchment skin

stretching fat and blue bone

outside the door

lay sun flowers air

she could not leave

her gadgets alone

with the right lighting

night yields a stage

to represent versions of ourselves

Brightness can blind us to darkness.

octopus heart

is helplessly floating

limbs cut off

every time it takes hold

craving toned light

and moods of night

starkness of day

revered in small doses

to ascertain the blackness of roses

now give me your life

as you swore solemnly

by the broken seal of my body

VI. DARKNESS

she made hooked followers
threads in her train
not turning around
as she walked through the flame

they say there are
more stars than sand
no fact of importance
for those who are drowning

in final surrender
to his calling
he would fight fire
with ice cold heart

sing to me
so it seems for a while
i closed my eyes
just to better listen

the loss of beauty
too painful yet
still all we can do
is find it anew

they censured the old homeless
for passing out graveyard flowers
deeming it more decent
to let beauty rot

VI. DARKNESS

deadly pains of life
foiling his mind to home
will he make it through this strife
or has he written his last poem

when hands hit herd halt you
through all your existence
they're hard to accept
as giving thereafter

locked safely inside
her heavy armor
she sank to the ground
in emotional seas

languid motions toward happiness
almost certain it is out of reach
still silent fury internally presses
sapping her energy like a leech

a piano rests
in a long-dead mansion
i start a few notes
then decide to stop

great many efforts
breaking his peace
were about making memories
the rest about disremembering

VI. DARKNESS

if you should become
detached from possessions
how much of a stranger
you'd be to yourself

black and white news reels
bellow insincerities
no everything was not alright then
glad we can't go back

suspicious of other people's agendas
wrapped up in chosen solitude
she's wondering i could die in here
no one even i would likely notice

she let herself go
to where she lost touch
with herself

most want to get
just by a life
exhausting them
without end

like a broken doll
who says nothing
only twitches
when the ring is pulled
some day possibly a grenade

VI. DARKNESS

she described
what it felt like
falling to death
her whole life

he hated songs
that made him walk shards
of his or other broken hearts

combat gear
left in the coat room
attending this dance
themed the softer side
stuck in defenses he cannot hide

since losing sixth sense
he stopped fighting the furies
that made him before
the fall battle thin air

the hardest thing
we are threatened to do
is burying a love
that's still alive

sadness is looking back
in a daydream
causing us pain
to keep and forget

VI. DARKNESS

sharp snapping splinters
of merciless ice
her heart melts
to water the flowers

the empty despair
she left in this room
still haunts me
after so many years

keeping you present
in imagination
embracing a ghost
walking through me

when hot rain and ashes

from burnt skies are falling

i'll wake with you

singing our love to sleep

such sorrow

i sometimes detect in her

she says that's because

of the life she wasted

they made a mannequin

of her body

headless torso

still carrying her name

VI. DARKNESS

forget it she quipped
and added this pain
to her list of facts to deny

she's not here today
got lost in the night
doing her best
projecting the bright
face mask of a stranger

petals of flowers disembodied
seemed like sensual violence
she'd rather leave them
to die on their own

you turn to me gently
and say something smiling
but i cannot hear you
as life races by

broken people
everywhere
breaking others
for pain to share

she gasps it chillingly concerns her
still after all these years of hearing
he went missing without explanation
hiding her wish to know of his death

VII.
POETIC ESSENCE

VII. POETIC ESSENCE

poems are clouds of wordy vapors
not taking their picture
they change formation
eventually disappear

how can we write
in lines of pink frosting
and not cover up
expanses of pain

i cannot wait
to hear the music
that must be playing
inside you

sometimes i fall in love with a poem
and my heart embraces
with all of its vessels
what my thinking mind
cannot quite comprehend

stop calling me your angel
i've fallen many times
a punch drunk fighter
who keeps getting up
to write about flying in rhymes

forlorn lands' last transmission pole
broadcasting bits of a human soul

VII. POETIC ESSENCE

birds don't cry
when sadness strikes
they know we rely on their music

played window open
lamenting love songs
daring the right heart
to walk on by

i venerate music
that charges me to sparks
moves me to tears
or sends shivers down my spine
all else is acoustic wallpaper

saturday evening

wine and olives

listening with you

to exotic cadence

outside reality

fades in our stories

banned from this candlelit cave

holding head stern

she will write about this

secret of suffering

keeping her captive

Poetry is real or imaginary honesty.

VII. POETIC ESSENCE

i fear we will run out of poetry soon
just like we ran out of music

he pondered strenuously
what he should write
to awaken her heart
from its sleeping potential

her words silent
their meaning screaming
frustration of being
hope she's merely getting started
and won't be thwarted
when her writing is discarded

i love about her

she sings with a passion

as if every song could be her last

lost in dreams

we stand in a forest

listen feel breathe

its moist fertile aura

arms stretched to heaven

humans and trees

the music they played

scrubbed my nerve endings raw

to open a sense for creation

VII. POETIC ESSENCE

practicing till my fingers bled
now i don't even know i'm playing
guitar absorbed all into her wine red
singing out loud what i try saying

every note i play for her
every tone i sing for him
that other people are also there
sometimes takes remembering

the rrr of guitar
is what i'm after
the way she responds
to my every touch

the song i wrote you
is all that survives
echoing empty halls
of my heart

every person
a piece of music
every music
related to light

remember this love song
from a long time ago
and the agony
we had not met yet

VII. POETIC ESSENCE

he always had planned
to write her a song
but stalled too long
their love went wrong

i walk the night
with music only i can hear
tomorrow
an airport door will open
releasing you into my arms

poetry is no dainty rhyming
it's a blinking eye
in the cyclone of life

telling stories

dispelling presumptions

reliving your life

finding your truth

keeping poems

short and brisk

for fear of being

drawn into them

writing a note to say with flowers

he could not love her any more

he failed to sever the last two words

and found his effects outside the door

VII. POETIC ESSENCE

stories written during the night
should not be judged by day

the ladies looked at me bewildered
like rabbits seeing a human eat grass

all my letters unraveled
swirling on pieces of soot
from the firestorm you are

her song is wondrously invasive
as if she knew passages to your heart

blue hour ghosts and shadows
dance in french-doored gardens
we watch spellbound inside
no sound no light

good poems are
like unfinished paintings
bad poems more
like coloring books

he one day will dare
devising a poem
that fits her
like a painted-on dress

VII. POETIC ESSENCE

rock and roll
reborn every time
music gives angry truth
cries for attention

since we met
my life has been set
to throngs of songs for you
scrambling my head

laying out poems
like stepping stones
hoping they one day
will lead her to him

our rhyme on this universe is
unraveling upon our reveling

my favorite words all beaten up
into stale wretched clichés

When words take on meanings we
imagine beyond their customary
event horizon, poetry arises in us.

a picture of you an unspoken poem
a life with you an unknown nirvana

VIII. ART OF LIFE

VIII. ART OF LIFE

gentle waves lapping
around my feet
scared with baby fish

i like night life best
when all patrons have left
and i play piano
for me and you

on the doorstep
of what she deems life
waiting to be let in
when all she needs
is around her

girl was taught grace
pacing books on her head
once she had read them
walked prouder yet

before we ask or judge
and before we recall
who and where we are
let us forget ourselves and love

aimless flutter till hitting a wall
existence remaining confounding
swallowed by superficialities' squall
drifting with shifting grounding

VIII. ART OF LIFE

life is not mystic
the oracle said
all you must do is
pay attention

thankful for books
when machined is our work
they lead us back
to good senses

Art does not have to be obviously
beautiful. It must offer alternative
reflections to existing views. Beauty
arises from the intrigue this causes.

with every act
tell yourself
it's limited

sitting on his wallet too long
he lost all feeling in leg and heart

the forest and the meadow
are reflections of our soul

he does not know how to love
just does it or better lets it happen

VIII. ART OF LIFE

people not giving what matters time
placing themselves or others in boxes

all that ever was is or will be
has only the import given by me
great potential for burden or freedom

tell me again for old times' sake
how much you tried to be found
then go on proudly to find your self
until your existence is sound
your life's statement's for you to make
define yourself by your give and take
leave no ambition shelved

we each decide

how much we let life wait

doomed if we fail

to honor our words

revere and mimic those

shedding tears and straining

for unknown troubled souls

people don't have time anymore

as if they were close to death

VIII. ART OF LIFE

forward thinking forward doing
heading toward the next precipice
to extend its ledge or build a bridge

sometimes the words
dissolve to fragments
broken crystal ball

so this was life
he had barely noticed
how it had flown
a film on fast forward
suddenly cut
before it made sense

give thanks to the love of flowers
each day rise to the sun reborn

endless regret and redemption hope
if we joined hands heads and hearts

recalling your past
say this was i
sense tension or acceptance

people ringing their bell so loud
they cannot hear the music

VIII. ART OF LIFE

You not only can't but should not try to please everybody. True harmony requires shared responsibility.

i am like air
stealing my tranquility
takes more than furious hitting me

what would you say
if the ground opened up
leaving you endlessly falling
would you lament
the apparent trap
or accept lightness as calling

be one of those
who have deeply felt
what the world
would want to say

he did not care
what day it was
as long as it was a day

this was so what
what is or will be
is open not shut
so take a leap
and skip your rut

VIII. ART OF LIFE

absurd to describe
a work of art
that already fully
expresses itself

when stricken by loss
take heart in the fact
that all is merely visiting

if people ignore
a beautiful soul
pity them for
being blind
to such matters

not as effective as we'd like to be
limited time tools skill energy
but we can do our best

all our problems arise
from lack of essentials
missing balance
or failed perception

how can we duly consider life
when much is amiss
robbing concentration
concentrate consideration on this
we must diligently and patient

VIII. ART OF LIFE

tormented

torn mended

scorn tended

thorn ended

love makes us live

the emotions of others

sometimes that thrills

but more often bothers

so we keep living afraid of love

two kinds of beauty

radiant flower

its appreciation

days months and years
are sifting away
with not much to show
in the colander

to comprehend
we must find truth
unaffected by desires
and thus first truth about desires

if we acknowledged unmet desires
took mutual gossip and judgment
and moved ahead from then on free
we might build authentic harmony

VIII. ART OF LIFE

when choosing directions
for your love
take care not to dim it in others

i'd like to boast life won't change me
except maybe death
which will freeze me in time
but then again to experience growth
i must let life change me
and change life both

when life's too unbearable
or beautiful to quietly take
that's when art springs forth

don't claim
you did anything
just for me
all we do
in a way is for us

the saving sad grace
of unaware lives
they are a matter of time

wasted times are like
spent paper towels
no sense attempting
to roll them back up

IX. TRUST AND DOUBT

IX. TRUST AND DOUBT

She entrusts herself to his protection. He is eager to earn her trust because she gives him cause to be brave. They subject themselves to power, trusting their support will engender care in return. Is this still how we behave?

when people tell me
i have not changed
i never know if it is praise

drifting between wide-ranging edges
and boring straight direction pledges
he never knew what path to take

her love makes him wish
he could cry and bleed
knowing he will be unscathed

she sought solitude's cool shadow
in the hot sunlight of his love

you the way she says it
the mood could go either way

her truth was similar to a comb
with several missing teeth

IX. TRUST AND DOUBT

he held her tight

in anonymous struggle

with everyone

offering open arms

she did not know what happened

bereft of energy to find out

what would it be good for anyway

except to mistrust a future love

no reason apparent

why they should meet

and still they felt

it was meant to happen

clasping each other

with all our might

still leaves potential for falling

fast slinking rope

that i might grasp

could burn my hands

don't know where it ends

falling risk vast

not giving up hope

having fought evil with hardened fists

for what seemed to him like a lifetime

could they open receiving her mildly

IX. TRUST AND DOUBT

the only time
it hurts loving you
is when you don't tell me
what is true

she let him know he had no reason
to ever fear her leaving him
except by cause of that fear

his arms around her in their sleep
feel lately much too heavy
he tries to pin down
a love he can't keep
her mind is made up already

too lonely to trust
the world was real

all i had was a sense to go there
thus we met and loved

all you need to find your path
you have already inside you

only those rare times
when everything's still
he's certain to be alive

IX. TRUST AND DOUBT

mind please recount me
why i should not love her
you're contradicting my senses

she thinks this is too beautiful
i'm sure i don't deserve it
he feels this is too perfect
it certainly cannot last

tired seclusion in her eyes
she tried to disguise
by fervent laughter
knew to ease him with her lies
to finally get what she was after

blinded to details
she turned to the sun
her warmth of love
shone undiminished

alternate universe suspicion
seemed to be all in his head
except that the grapefruit juice
read rugby red

i am less upset
about what you did
than that i must live
remembering it

IX. TRUST AND DOUBT

hearing her sing
i began to believe
that this realm was built
from love and vibration

he was more at ease
with machines' innocent detachment
even in their malfunctions

i can't hide from love
it may play coy when i pursue it
test my mettle question motives
but when it senses i avoid it
it comes after and taunts me

all we hold

we eventually crush

better to touch invite wait for return

he was most worried

about his possessions

the kind of home

they would have

when he's gone

switch wine

of cheap and expensive bottles

watch people lie

to themselves and others

IX. TRUST AND DOUBT

she deemed him at present
her most precious asset
though she had others
tempting replacement

if you have me feeling love
in the morning
as much as you are tonight
i will forget all rational warning
and simply trust it will be alright

most people are whelmed
by their mantra of right
not entertaining anything else

succumb in flattery
or heed her ban
he would not stand for it
proving a man

god please do not hate me
after all i'm the way you made me
i made you to vent my frustration
that all i do ends in consummation

he does not trust her
without reason
their love's not lasting
past the season

IX. TRUST AND DOUBT

when it gets still when time is up
when we are stuck or run out of luck
when we had our fill and get the bill
are we more than future has-beens

she dares not say
what she feels today
they would not understand
some time soon
she'll have the sway
to overcome their judgment

when your life is like a nightmare
question whether you're conscious

she has all the pieces
but not in their places
whatever she says
prompts puzzled faces

with him she had trespassed
limits set for any other man
uncertain where this would take her
and fearing to never or ever return

he impressed her as interesting
and confessed she was beguiling
unclear what to make of the other
or whether to keep an open mind

IX. TRUST AND DOUBT

your disarming purity my love
has me afraid of the thereafter

the right mix between
un and predictable

it's easy to be virtuous
when you're too boring
to lure temptation

she says i always think about you
i'd like to give her good reason

all her six senses
were clap trap certain
he was the one
she was searching for

the problem with you is
i never know
how you can be
so angry with me

the way she puts her armor on
makes me wonder about her day
night's tenderness is almost gone
an absent kiss and she's away

IX. TRUST AND DOUBT

i know you she said
as if to cut off
any chance for his redemption

i put my emotions
in your hands
never so scared
for my life before

she shuns me for being a man
resenting her implication
wanting her warmth
i tried to prove her wrong
but she hates that even more

he was named

he was called

he refused

he was framed

was denounced

to be shamed

yet stood tall

never tamed

she makes him feel

just like he wanted

he seems the hunter

she the hunted

he won't suspect

it's the other way

why are men such easy prey

IX. TRUST AND DOUBT

when we feel nothing
needs saying
should we be glad for that

one moment she's loving
the next catatonic
he tries to get through
she takes offense
persuaded he's guilty
he makes amends

i know choosing me
you left many unseen
i better not raise any doubt

saying my name
and embracing me
you inspire new life
free spirit granting honor

you wear and do things
that are now in fashion
how can i be sure
i'm not one of them

back then you told me all about him
to warn me not to behave like that
but lately you fondly recite his name
as if i were only a pawn in your game

X.
FICTION
AND
REALITY

X. FICTION AND REALITY

beneath her shy and tenderness
rests fury i had to awake

they though telling each other to go
held on tightly belying such words

shoreline hazed in wayward dreams
clearing imagined locations

not what she had hoped for
he was his own
she would have to compromise

no prince or white knight
she thought she wanted
those fairytale memes
she long ago shunted
what then was last night
this dream he still haunted

tell him again
how you'll never leave
so he can take you for granted

we all sell something maybe so
but she sells herself at a price too low
for fear there won't be bidders

X. FICTION AND REALITY

ahead we would go separate ways
so we profess liking how it stays

morning till evening
they were together
even the night
offered little escape

went out into the rain
pretending he could cry
walked hours in the cold
to see if he could die
wished he had not been told
and it were all a lie

he a tortured burl from the ground
she a translucent elegant insect

her love has infected him already
little else more to do than wait

four in the mornings
he fancied a bite
teatime for vampires

at the end of our days
all pretenses will be lost

X. FICTION AND REALITY

her allure
plush like a cloud
false appearance
of cuddling him

he was supposed to be her prince
and for this reason has ever since
tried to be noble like that
in a world that lacks heart and tact

quiet reflection of life
disturbs her
she craves drama
distracting herself

trolls on forest strolls with their mate
turned by magic mushrooms they ate
beautiful luminous light winged elves
taking night flights in that fairy state
lapsing at dawn back into themselves

she loved me wanting
to make up for time
we were and would be apart

that pause in life
we are just here
together
in silent intent

X. FICTION AND REALITY

let us not speak
of the size of our love
we'd only debase
the abyss we feel

they threatened expulsion
if she won't stop crying
in history class

winged traveler of ages
shielding her secrets for long
soon must go on
if she won't respond
opening her cages

sweet dream of a
pastry shop ballerina
behind the counter
her smile at first fake
our eyes share a glance
then she starts to dance
black and white swan in a lake
i swim in her wake
forget about cake
until i wistfully awake

a longing grip into emptiness
where her hair
once caressed his hand
she had claimed to be a princess
escaped from a foreign land

X. FICTION AND REALITY

trying his utmost not to hurt her
with silent laconic roughness
accustomed to battling dragons

wild times
we spent in tight embrace
inhaling each other's breath
until we almost suffocated

she will do as he desires
as long as he acts
within her approval
he'll go along
to save face and dodge mires

When I was little, I was often invited
as the only boy to girls' parties since I
did not play rough. Along the way,
this feature must have lost attraction.

imagine an idyllic setting
in which you can live happily
now tell yourself that story
and make it reality

she felt his blood pulsate inside her
tingling and tinging her every nerve
as she had longed for inviting his bite
a prize truly worth avoiding sun light

X. FICTION AND REALITY

the lies about christmas
we buy and sell others
make us more desperate
in sugar glazed covers
during its fleeting truce

her love does have conditions
her strength patience pardon an end
he brings out these natural limits
and guilt for not being a saint

she had no compunctions
to pop his bubbles
as soon as he could blow them

why don't you get lost
in our storybook
allow me to find you
awaken our love

reality we imagine to be
conducting ourselves accordingly
may anticipate a better state
resulting harm may also be great
better to differentiate

tired of touting love and beauty
or longing to be extolled for them
she made a point of merely being

X. FICTION AND REALITY

what if the nightmares
playing inside
are true reflections
of real events

he had no more wife
but was a farmer
who had accepted
the earth as his bride

tired of life
in which artifice killed her
she wants nature pure
without filler or filter

my life story

is much about someone

refusing increasingly

not to exist

love lays a trap to expect perfection

by anticipation and ardent throws

its true proof comes at dissatisfaction

in compromise for common goals

to call her divine

describes barely half

the depth of her love

or wrath for betrayal

X. FICTION AND REALITY

she does not want to go to sleep
because of all sadness it will keep
except a false overnight sensation
that morning grants inauguration

anonymity potentials of social media
enable people to be anybody
even themselves

daisy-chaining supercomputers
to figure out
a path to peace
and all they came up with
was the picture of a flower

her sheer loveliness
pulls me up into realms
that make this appear
a magical world

she used to lose track
of conversations
whenever she shifted
a gear in her car

nothing's ever really over
until synapses unwind
echoes of what was
play on in our mind

X. FICTION AND REALITY

he first took recordings of the past
by calculating refractions
then found his insights presented vast
prospects for curative actions

after the fall
they planned to thrive
a new beginning
without old mistakes

i hate i get lost when you're not there
instead of remaining your rock
so i pretend you need my care
and protection 'round the clock

you think all men
are artlessly predictable
but i will not look at you
without my heart

the memories of pain with her
stalk him like dark forest shadows
only a new love's bright burning light
can place him in flowering meadows

you think and feel too much
you're told even by yourself
will you come to your senses
and learn to dim them to cope

www.ingramcontent.com/pod-product-compliance
Lightning Source LLC
Chambersburg PA
CBHW032109090426
42743CB00007B/292